Pebble® Plus

Rain

SCHOOL OF EDUCATION
CURRICULUM LABORATORY
UM-DEARBORN

by Erin Edison

Consulting Editor: Gail Saunders-Smith, PhD

CAPSTONE PRESS
a capstone imprint

Pebble Plus is published by Capstone Press,
151 Good Counsel Drive, P.O. Box 669, Mankato, Minnesota 56002.
www.capstonepub.com

Books published by Capstone Press are manufactured with paper
containing at least 10 percent post-consumer waste.

Library of Congress Cataloging-in-Publication Data
Edison, Erin.
 Rain / by Erin Edison.
  p. cm.—(Pebble plus. Weather basics)
 Summary: "Simple text and full-color photographs describe rain and its role in the water cycle"—Provided by
publisher.
 Includes bibliographical references and index.
 ISBN 978-1-4296-6055-6 (library binding)
 ISBN 978-1-4296-7079-1 (paperback)
 1. Rain and rainfall—Juvenile literature. 2. Hydrologic cycle—Juvenile literature. I. Title. II. Series.
 QC924.7.E35 2012
 551.57'7—dc22   2010053973

Editorial Credits
Erika L. Shores, editor; Kyle Grenz, designer; Laura Manthe, production specialist

Photo Credits
Alamy: C.O. Mercial, 21, Dave Chapman, 13; Getty Images Inc.: Tim Boyle, 17; Shutterstock: Andrew Chin, cover,
Attila Huszti, 1, Claudio Rossol, 11, dpaint, 7, dutourdumonde, 15, Marcelo Dufflocq W., 5, Mona Makela, back cover,
Nixx Photography, 19, SebStock, 9

Artistic Effects
Shutterstock: marcus55

**Capstone Press thanks Mike Shores, earth science teacher at RBA Public Charter School in Mankato,
 Minnesota, for his assistance on this book.**

Note to Parents and Teachers

The Weather Basics series supports national science standards related to earth science. This
book describes and illustrates rain. The images support early readers in understanding the
text. The repetition of words and phrases helps early readers learn new words. This book
also introduces early readers to subject-specific vocabulary words, which are defined in the
Glossary section. Early readers may need assistance to read some words and to use the Table of
Contents, Glossary, Read More, Internet Sites, and Index sections of the book.

Printed in the United States of America in North Mankato, Minnesota.
032011   006110CGF11

Table of Contents

What Is Rain?

Rain is water that falls

from clouds.

It helps plants grow.

It makes puddles.

Rain brings water

to living things. Rain fills

lakes where fish live.

Plants use water in the ground.

The Water Cycle

Rain starts as water on
the ground. Water in lakes
and oceans evaporates.
Water vapor rises into the sky.

In the air, water vapor cools.

It turns into liquid droplets.

This is called condensation.

Droplets stick to tiny particles

in the air. Then clouds form.

Droplets in the clouds grow

and become heavier than air.

Rain falls. This process

is called precipitation.

13

Evaporation, condensation, and precipitation are the water cycle's three parts. Water evaporates, makes clouds, then falls to the ground. This pattern happens again and again.

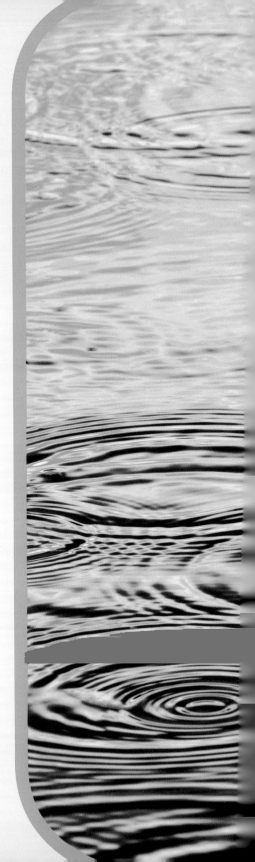

Floods and Droughts

When too much rain falls,
water covers places
it normally doesn't. This is
called a flood. Floods damage
roads, crops, and buildings.

Droughts happen when
too little rain falls.
Rivers and lakes dry up.
Soil becomes hard. Plants and
animals die without water.

Too much or too little rain
can hurt living things.
Animals, people, and plants
need just enough rain.

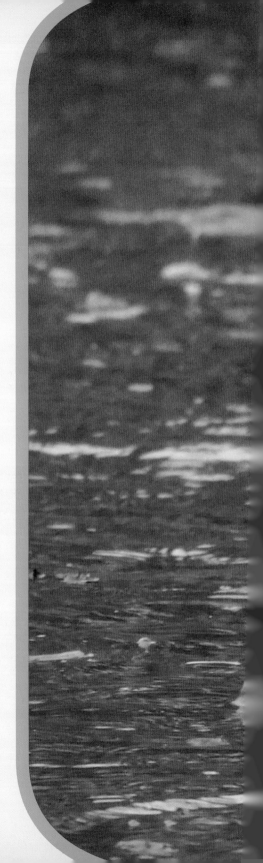

Glossary

condensation—the act of turning from a gas into a liquid

crop—a plant grown in large amounts; crops usually are grown for food

drought—a long period of weather with little or no rainfall

evaporate—the action of a liquid changing into a gas; heat causes water to evaporate

flood—to overflow with water

particle—a tiny piece of something; water droplets stick to dust, salt, and other tiny particles in the air to form clouds

water vapor—water in the form of a gas; water vapor is made of tiny bits of water that cannot be seen

Read More

Goldsmith, Mike. *The Weather.* Now We Know About. New York: Crabtree Pub., 2010.

Higginson, Sheila Sweeny. *Drip, Drop! The Rain Won't Stop!* Your Turn, My Turn Reader. New York: Simon Spotlight, 2010.

Salas, Laura Purdie. *Colors of Weather.* Colors All Around. Mankato, Minn.: Capstone Press, 2011.

Internet Sites

FactHound offers a safe, fun way to find Internet sites related to this book. All of the sites on FactHound have been researched by our staff.

Here's all you do:

Visit *www.facthound.com*

Type in this code: 9781429660556

Check out projects, games and lots more at
www.capstonekids.com

Index

Word Count: 180
Grade: 1
Early-Intervention Level: 18